SPACE MATTERS

Written by
Jacque Lynn

Illustrated by
Lydia Nichols

CLARION BOOKS
Houghton Mifflin Harcourt
Boston   New York

Spaces matter.

Theyhelpmakesenseofsentences

and to see

the whole

picture.

Without spaces,
cities would be just one big block,

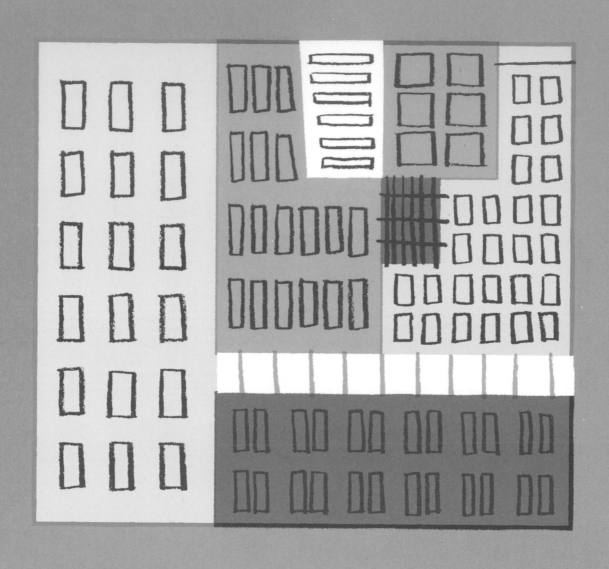

and echoes, impossible.

But make some space
and find a new friend,

or a hiding spot.
Quick!

Watch a big space turn into little ones—
a sky full of white is now snowflakes,

and a sea of blue,

a snug abode.

Feel a pause—

that space

between moments

to make a wish—

turn a

into a

beat

beat beat

beat

and

Ready

is even more exciting.

Spaces keep pudding from tasting of pickles.

Yuck!

And noodles from slipping away.

Oops!

A space in play shows where to put your foot down,

or to place an *X* or *O*.

Three in a row!

A sudden gap lets in light
and can chase dark skies away.

It keeps the tooth fairy in business

or makes room for something new.

All day, spaces make sense
of the world around us,

until lights-out makes space to dream!

For those who look and truly listen,
especially you, Tommy —J.L.

To Julia, for giving me space —L.N.

Clarion Books
3 Park Avenue
New York, New York 10016

Clarion Books is an imprint of Houghton Mifflin Harcourt Publishing Company.

hmhbooks.com

The illustrations in this book are mixed media finished digitally.
The text was set in Gotham Rounded.
Book design by Mary Claire Cruz and Lydia Nichols

Library of Congress Cataloging-in-Publication Data

Names: Lynn, Jacque, author. | Nichols, Lydia, illustrator.
Title: Space matters / by Jacque Lynn ; illustrated by Lydia Nichols.
Description: Boston ; New York : Clarion Books, Houghton Mifflin Harcourt,
    [2020] | Audience: Ages 4 to 7. | Audience: Grades K–1. | Summary: From
    the spaces between words in a sentence to the vast, blue sky, spaces,
    both large and small, add beauty and make sense of the world around us.
Identifiers: LCCN 2019039944 | ISBN 9781328801470 (hardcover) |
    ISBN 9780358378563 (ebook)
Subjects: CYAC: Space—Fiction.
Classification: LCC PZ7.1.L954 Sp 2020 | DDC [E]—dc23
LC record available at https://lccn.loc.gov/2019039944

Manufactured in China
SCP 10 9 8 7 6 5 4 3 2 1
4500799775